Yoga Birds

Maddy Wagler

Zea Books, Lincoln, Nebraska

Yoga Birds

ISBN 978-1-60962-162-9

Zea Books are publisehd by the University of Nebraska-Lincoln Libraries

Eletronic (pdf) edition available online at http://digitalcommons.unl.edu/zeabooks/

Print edition avaialable from http://www.lulu.com/spotlight/unlib

for Fox, Ash, and Winter

Mom says,
Yoga is for the birds.

We're not bird-brained
or winging it.
We're eagle-eyed and wise.

That's why we call, *Look Mom!*
and show her our eagle.

Why?
We're not clay pigeons
or pigeon-eyed.

We like the crow's feet
of our mom's smile.

That's why we call, *Look Mom!*
and show her our pigeon.

**Why?
We're early birds
and birds of a feather.**

That's why we call, *Look Mom!*
And show her our stork.

**Why?
We sing like crows,
all ruffled and kerfuffled.**

That's why we call
Look Mom!
and show her our swan dive.

Why?
We're posers and peacocks
ready to preen.

That's why we call
Look Mom!
and show her our crow.

We grow taller and call
Look Mom!
and show her our crane.

**Why?
We're a flock together
under Mom's roost.**

When Mom says
Let's Fly.

we save other poses
like sunbird
for next time.

Why?
We're under her wing
and she's under ours too.

**That's why we breathe
and say, *Namaste*
and she says it too.**

Author's Note

Yoga is a Sanskrit word that means "union" or "yoke." It brings together the mind and body. It connects breath with posture and presence with awareness. The practice of yoga began in ancient India. Many styles have since developed. Traditionally, poses or "asanas" are taught in Sanskrit to deepen a yoga practice. By including Sanskrit, it's the hope that young yoga students will develop language skills as they build strength, flexibility, balance, and mind-body awareness from the practice.

This book is designed to be shared by parents, instructors, or caregivers and children. It can be read aloud. Experiencing the postures can be part of the play. Additional asana instructions follow. When practicing yoga, it's important to pay attention to the feelings in the muscles and to only go to a good stretch. Remember to listen to the body, have fun and be playful with the poses, and breathe.

The journey of yoga can begin at any age. To further deepen a yoga practice, seek guidance, support, and instruction from qualified instructors. Exercise studios often design yoga classes specifically for children. To learn more about the practice of yoga, seek out resources from local libraries, fitness studios, and educational centers. Good materials can be online.

Namasté is a word that means the "light in me sees the light in you" or "I bow to you." When namasté is said at the end of a yoga practice, it means we bow to one another with respect, honor, and gratitude. It is one way we acknowledge the compassion, kindness, and love within each of us.

Namasté. And may your yoga journey be one of joy.

Kind Regards,
Maddy

Eagle
Garudasana

From standing, cross left elbow under right, palms together. Elbows up. Shoulders down. Bend knees. Shift weight to right foot. Cross left leg over right. Balance and breathe. Stand to release. Repeat other side.

Stork
Ardha padangushthasana

From standing, shift weight to right foot. Bend left leg. Lift it parallel to the ground. Reach arms overhead. Balance and breathe. Return to standing. Repeat other side.

Pigeon
Kapotasana

From all fours, bring right knee forward and straighten left leg. Sqaure hips. Walk hands towards hips. Lengthen spine. Hold and breathe. Return to all fours. Repeat other side.

Swan Dive
from *Surya Namaskar*

From standing, sweep arms up like wings on the inhale. On the exhale, sweep arms down and with soft knees and a flat back, fold forward. From the fold, sweep arms up with soft knees and a flat back, return to standing. Repeat a few times, moving on the breath.

Crow
Kakasana

From a squat, place palms on the ground. Make starfish fingers. Press knees into upper arms. With a strong core, lift hips and heels. Rock back and forth, then balance and breathe. Return to a squat.

www.ingramcontent.com/pod-product-compliance
Lightning Source LLC
Chambersburg PA
CBHW042011080426
42734CB00002B/47